TILL DEATH DO US PART

by

Billy Van Zandt

&

Jane Milmore

SAMUEL FRENCH, INC.

45 WEST 25TH STREET   NEW YORK 10010
7623 SUNSET BOULEVARD HOLLYWOOD 90046
LONDON   TORONTO

IMPORTANT BILLING AND CREDIT REQUIREMENTS

Cover Photo by Danny Sanchez.
Cover photo clockwise from top: Kathy Cagney, Michael J, Kroll, Sally Vold Winters, Glenn Jones, Eric Anderson, Jane Milmore, Sherle Tallent, Billy Van Zandt.

Till Death Do Us Part opened at the Henderson Theatre, Lincroft, New Jersey, May 18, 1990. It was produced by Mark Fleming and directed by Billy Van Zandt. Set design was by Chad Heulitt. Lighting design by Joseph Rembisz. Costume design by Kitty Cleary. The Stage Manager was Neil Murphy. Lights and special effects by Daniel J. Wojcik. Photography by Danny Sanchez. Sound engineers were Bob Guild, Michael Xenakis and Sue Kulinyi. Stage Crew: Ruth Calia, Debbie Case, Thomas J. Ceballos, Ian Gonzalez, and Cecil Sprung. Assistant to Van Zandt & Milmore was Kathleen Milmore. General Manager was Mary Ann Schulz. Box Office by Sharon McGoldrick and Pat Fleming. The cast, in order of appearance, was as follows:

SAM CRUMM	Drew Hollywood
ALAN	Eric Anderson
VICKIE	Jane Milmore
HAL	Glenn Jones
RHONDA	Sally Vold Winters
BUD	Michael J. Kroll
LINDA	Kathy Cagney
MITCHELL	Billy Van Zandt
FRAN	Sherle Tallent
PEARL EARLE	Jackie Neill
JEB	Art Neill

ACT I

(We see slides of four couples getting married, as "Chapel in the Moonlight"*plays. They are cliche wedding shots of cutting the cake, waving goodbye, toasting, etc. As the music ends, a spotlight is cast upon a middle-aged man DC. It is SAM CRUMM, our narrator.)

SAM. Ah, young love. It makes life worth living, doesn't it? Puts a bouncy spring in your step. A rosy color in your cheek. A little sparkle in your eye. They looked so innocent up there, didn't they? So full of joy and hope and passion. Those poor, ignorant bastards. Oh, forgive me for not introducing myself. I'm Sam Crumm. I'm a bachelor. You? You're the audience. What? Me? Cynical? Perhaps, but I wasn't always this way. The story you're about to see is true. You may know many of these people. In fact, they may be you. But, let's start at the beginning. Back when love was new and times were simpler. Back before stolen glances turned into sullen glares. Before pet names were replaced by foul curse words and broken bric-a-brac.

---

* See cautionary note in front matter.

(LIGHTS up on ALAN and VICKIE, on a park bench DL. HE holds a bouquet of flowers.)

SAM. Meet Alan and Vickie. They loved each other. Blindly. You know couples like this. So in love they never notice they have absolutely nothing in common. You know, like, she's a democrat, he's republican. She likes movies with Woody Allen, he likes movies where naked prison girls wrestle in the shower. She remembers every detail of their life together. And he remembers ... absolutely nothing at all.

(SPOTLIGHT out on Sam Crumm.)

ALAN. For you, my sweet.
VICKIE. For me?
ALAN. Nobody else but.
VICKIE. Oh, Alan. They're beautiful.
ALAN. Not as beautiful as you.
VICKIE. How did you know I loved lilies?
ALAN. They match your oh so beautiful eyes.
VICKIE. But my eyes aren't blue.
ALAN. What?
VICKIE. Lilies are blue. My eyes are green, silly.
ALAN. Oh. I meant ... the stems.
VICKIE. *(SHE giggles.)* At least you remembered it was our anniversary.

(As THEY embrace, ALAN reacts. The LIGHTS dim. SPOTLIGHT comes back up on Sam DC.)

SAM. Hal and Rhonda. They were inseparable. They couldn't keep their hands off each other.

(LIGHTS up on HAL and RHONDA DR. THEY are in bed frozen in a kiss.)

SAM. They were practically joined at the hip. And a good portion of the time, that's exactly how'd you'd find them.

(SPOTLIGHT out on Sam.)

(RHONDA leans over and marks something in a red diary.)

HAL. What's that? What are you doing, Love Puppet?
RHONDA. This? I'm adding to my sex list.
HAL. Your what?
RHONDA. My sex list. See? Everytime we make love I mark it in this little book.
HAL. That is so adorable. How long have you been doing that?
RHONDA. Since the first time. We've made love six hundred and twelve times since we got married.

HAL. Really? You keep track of that? That's so ... cute.

RHONDA. *You're* so cute.

HAL. You're cuter.

RHONDA. You're cutest.

HAL. You're cute-est-er.

RHONDA. I think the number's going to go up again tonight.

HAL. (*Kissing her.*) Let's see if we can hit an even thou' by Arbor Day.

RHONDA. (*Stopping him.*) And look, we've made love in exactly fourteen different beds.

HAL. Wow.

RHONDA. Six different cars. Four different parks. Two phone booths. Twelve movie theaters. Five alleys. Twenty-nine pools. And two Seven-Elevens.

HAL. I love you for recording all this.

RHONDA. It's a history book of our love. All our thoughts and desires.

HAL. It's a Pulitzer Prize Winner.

RHONDA. Look, it's even got pictures.

HAL. Wow. You drew that?

RHONDA. Mm-hmm.

HAL. It's so cute!

RHONDA. Thank you.

HAL. Is that me?

RHONDA. No, it's Mel Gibson.

HAL. The movie actor?

RHONDA. I fantasized about him last Tuesday. Is that naughty of me?

HAL. Oh, no. That's so adorable that you would think it's naughty. Who's that?

RHONDA. Tommy Lasorda.

HAL. You little devil-woman. You know how much I love baseball!

RHONDA. You're not mad?

HAL. How could I be mad? (*Pointing to another drawing.*) Clark Gable?

RHONDA. Shemp Howard.

(*On Hal's perplexed look, the LIGHTS fade. The SPOTLIGHT comes back up on Sam Crumm DC.*)

SAM. Bud and Linda. A perfectly matched pair. You know the type. She wears a green shirt. He has to wear matching green pants. She loves to cook. He loves to eat.

(*LIGHTS up on Bud and Linda DR.*)

SAM. She finds his weaknesses attractive. And he, well, he enjoys being weak.

(*SPOTLIGHT out on Sam.*)

BUD. Honey, I'm home.
LINDA. You poor overworked thing.

(*BUD and LINDA kiss hello.*)

LINDA. What's wrong? You look pale.

BUD. Oh, there was a draft in the office. I missed you.

LINDA. I missed you more.

(*THEY kiss. HE sneezes.*)

BUD. Excuse me.

LINDA. God bless you.

BUD. Thank you.

LINDA. (*Teasing.*) I have good news.

BUD. (*Ecstatic.*) Did the new mattress arrive?

LINDA. Yes! And guess what? It's super firm for your problem back!

(*THEY jump up and down.*)

BUD. Hooray! You always think of me.

LINDA. That's my whole life, thinking about you. Now you get yourself into a hot tub right this minute, young man.

BUD. If you say so. Will you come and scrub my back?

LINDA. I always do.

BUD. You're so good to me.

LINDA. That's what I'm here for!

BUD. (*Sniffles.*) Tissue...

LINDA. "Tissue?" I hardly know you!

(*THEY giggle obnoxiously. LIGHTS dim. SPOTLIGHT up on Sam.*)

SAM. Ooh, are they in for a fall. Mitchell and Fran. Gaga in love. There's something about that first stage of puppy love, that well ... it just makes you want to gaga. Imagine yourself sitting in some restaurant, about to put a fork full of liver to your lips...and seeing this from across the room:

(*LIGHTS up on an unattractive young couple, FRAN and MITCHELL, gaga in love. THEY stare dreamily into each others eyes. THEY feed each other cake in baby talk during the following.*)

MITCHELL. I missed you today.
FRAN. Not as much as I missed you.
MITCHELL. Bet I did.
FRAN. Did not.
MITCHELL. I t'ought of you awl day.
FRAN. Did you weall-wy?
MITCHELL. Mm-hmm.
FRAN. Come on, one more bite.
MITCHELL. I can't.
FRAN. Please? For me.
MITCHELL. For you? Mm ... Okay. (*Eats the cake.*)
FRAN. Is it good?
MITCHELL. Mm-hmm! (*Takes a fork full and tries to feed Fran.*)
MITCHELL. Now you have to have a bite for me.

FRAN. Well, okay. (*Takes the cake. And eats it.*)

FRAN. I want a bigger bite than that, Mr. Baker Man.

MITCHELL. Okay. Here you go. Open wide for the Super Chief. (*Makes train noises as HE feeds her another bite.*)

FRAN. Mm. It tastes so good. Now you.

MITCHELL. I can't. I weal-wy can't.

FRAN. Pwease? Pwetty pwease for your wifey-woofy-honey-dolly?

MITCHELL. Okay. If my wifey weally wants me to.

(*SHE feeds him. HE can barely swallow it.*)

MITCHELL. Now you. One more.
FRAN. Only if you have one more.
MITCHELL. We'll *both* have one more.

(*THEY share a big bite of cake.*)

MITCHELL. Fwan?
FRAN. Yes, Mitchell?
MITCHELL. I tink I'm gonna fwo up.

(*LIGHTS dim. SPOTLIGHT on Sam.*)

SAM. You and me both, pal. And, no offense, but I don't even want to see *attractive* people doing that. Why is it, something that starts out so new and exciting can become so routine and mundane? Maybe it's 'cause you know she's gonna be there day in, day out, winter, summer, spring and fall, year after year after year after year. And after a while, it gets real easy to take someone for granted. (*To man in audience.*) Am I right, sir? Sooner or later you'll find you just blend right into the background. Like another piece of furniture. And let's face it. Nobody wants to have sex with a wing chair. (*Re: Guy in audience.*) Well, except for that guy. Soon you'll find you know each other so well, you never have to finish a sentence. You never have to voice an actual opinion. In fact, you never have to do much of anything at all.

(*SPOTLIGHT out on Sam, as LIGHTS come up on Alan and Vickie's bedroom. HE reads "Presumed Innocent." SHE wears a sexy nightgown.*)

VICKIE. We never make love anymore.
ALAN. Sure we do.
VICKIE. (*After SHE thinks.*) When?
ALAN. Lots of times.
VICKIE. When?
ALAN. All those times.
VICKIE. What times?
ALAN. I just told you.
VICKIE. I can't remember the last time.
ALAN. What?
VICKIE. I said I can't remember the last time.
ALAN. What last time?

VICKIE. The last time we made love.

ALAN. What about it?

VICKIE. When was it?

ALAN. Your birthday.

VICKIE. My birthday?

ALAN. Yeah.

VICKIE. My birthday was six months ago.

ALAN. Whatever.

VICKIE. Doesn't that strike you as odd?

ALAN. How do you mean? It was your birthday, for Christ's Sake. If we didn't do it then, I never would have heard the end of it.

VICKIE. Six months, Alan. That's one hundred and eighty days. In dog time, that's three and a half years.

ALAN. (*Setting down book.*) Oh, I get it. You want to make love? Is that what this is all about, Miss Subtlety? Okay. We'll make love.

VICKIE. Well, I don't want to like that.

ALAN. You just said you wanted to.

VICKIE. Well, I do, but can't we have a little romance? How about saying "I love you" first?

ALAN. Okay! I love you!

VICKIE. You don't mean it.

ALAN. I mean it! I love you! I love you! I love you! Now are we going to do this or not?

VICKIE. Not with that attitude we're not.

ALAN. Look, either you want to or you don't. I don't really care one way or the other. I've had a long day.

VICKIE. Oh, and I suppose I've been out dancing all day.

ALAN. Hey, I was sitting here reading. You brought this up. I was perfectly content reading my book.

VICKIE. Okay, I want to.

ALAN. Okay. (*Then.*) Let me just finish this page.

VICKIE. (*Takes the book away and puts it down.*) You can finish it later.

ALAN. Hey, you lost my place!

VICKIE. I'm sorry.

ALAN. Dammit. You lose your place in a murder mystery, you might as well not even read it at all.

VICKIE. (*Tosses the book at Alan.*) Here. Read your book.

ALAN. I thought we were going to make love.

VICKIE. I changed my mind.

ALAN. Fine. (*Angrily picks his book up and starts to read.*)

VICKIE. Oh, and by the way ... the wife did it.

(*On his reaction, the LIGHTS fade. SPOTLIGHT on Sam.*)

SAM. She's right. I read the book. I noticed that we have a lot of married people here in the audience tonight. I can tell because, well, you're facing away from each other. When exactly do you realize you've hit your first rut? Do you ever see it coming, or do you just wake up one day and say, "What the hell is that?" To break the monotony, some couples take up wind surfing, some take up jazz-ercise, and some people ... well ... they go to other extremes.

(*SPOTLIGHT out on Sam. LIGHTS up in Hal and Rhonda's bedroom. RHONDA is on the bed, in a negligee. HAL is dressed in boxer shorts, a cape, and a batman mask. HE ties her to the headboard with scarves. There is a big thick red book next to the bed.*)

HAL. (*As HE ties Rhonda to the bed.*) Are you sure about this?
     RHONDA. Yes. It'll put a little zip into things.
     HAL. Where are the kids?
     RHONDA. They're asleep. Come on!
     HAL. I'm wearing a mask. I feel like a fool.
     RHONDA. Hal. What's the day today?
     HAL. Friday.
     RHONDA. And...
     HAL. You get to choose on Fridays. I get to choose on Saturdays. Okay. (*SHE is tied up.*) Now what am I supposed to do?
     RHONDA. Hal, we discussed this. Get up on the bureau and swoop down on me.
     HAL. I feel like a fool.
     RHONDA. It's my night to pick. You got to be the cheerleader coach last week.
     HAL. I know, but all I had to wear was a whistle. I didn't have to wear a cape. I didn't have to climb any bureaus. I didn't have to wear my son's rubber boots.

RHONDA. Start climbing.

HAL. All right, but tomorrow we get to play "The Plant Lady" and "The Janitor."

RHONDA. Okay. But tonight's my night. Get up there.

HAL. (*Climbs the bureau.*) Okay. Ready?

RHONDA. Yes! (*Acting.*) Oh, where can Batman be? The Joker has me tied to this sawmill. Where is Batman! Save me! Somebody, save me!

HAL. (*Reluctantly.*) I am here, Robin! I'm Batman.

RHONDA. Holy Sexual Gratification!

HAL. Don't worry, Boy Wonder. I'll have you down the Batpole in no time! (*HAL trips and falls off the bureau behind the bed.*)

HAL. Ah!!

RHONDA. Hal? Hal? Hal, are you all right? (*SHE is tied and can't get up.*)

RHONDA. Hal? Hal? (*SHE thinks, calls.*) Kids!?

(*LIGHTS fade. SPOTLIGHT on Sam.*)

SAM. The sad thing, is no matter how hard you try to jazz up your marriage, eventually there comes the day when you find her cute little voice becomes an irritating buzzing in your ear. The way he scrapes his ice cream bowl suddenly makes you want to scream. And even worse ... eccentric behavior becomes a major pain in the ass.

(*SPOTLIGHT out on Sam. LIGHTS up in the bedroom of Bud and Linda. LINDA reclines seductively on the bed. BUD stands away from her, clearing his sinuses.*)

LINDA. (*Purring like a cat.*) Make love to me.

BUD. (*Pounding his blocked ears.*) You talking to me?

LINDA. I said (*Purrs.*) make love to me!

BUD. (*Smiles, goes to kiss her and sneezes in ther face.*) Sorry.

LINDA. That's okay.

(*SHE wipes her face off and blots his. THEY go to kiss again. HE sneezes in her face again.*)

LINDA. Bud, stop it.

BUD. I'm sorry, I ... Are you wearing perfume?

LINDA. No. Oh, I am. I'm sorry. I am. I forgot, Bud.

(*BUD backs away and looks at her aghast.*)

LINDA. I was in Macy's and the girl shot me with a sample of Giorgio. I'm sorry, Bud. I'll wash it off.

BUD. (*Sneezes.*) It's okay. I want you so bad.

(*THEY kiss. HE starts scratching his stomach. Then his back.*)

LINDA. And I want you.

BUD. (*HE breaks apart to scratch.*) Is that ... polyester?

LINDA. (*Heated up.*) What?

BUD. Your nightgown. Is that polyester?

LINDA. (*Kissing him all over.*) It's synthetic silk.

BUD. (*He sneezes and scratches.*) Linda, I'm allergic to polyester.

LINDA. It's only forty percent polyester.

BUD. I know, but ... I'm getting rashy.

LINDA. I'll just take it off. (*SHE goes to remove her nightgown.*)

BUD. No, Linda. Don't. The particles will fly through the air. It'll spread all over. We'll have to vacuum. I'll just ... it's okay. Kiss me. (*H E sneezes.*)

LINDA. I'll open a window.

BUD. It's fine. It's going away. It's fine.

(*THEY kiss.*)

LINDA. Mm. Make love to me.

(*THEY sit on the bed and start to kiss.*)

BUD. Oh. Oh. Wait. My lip!

LINDA. Your what?

BUD. My lip is swelling up. (*HE scratches his chest. His lip swells up.*)

BUD. Were you drinking wine today?

LINDA. Yes. I had a glass at lunch.

BUD. (*HE sneezes.*) I'm allergic to wine.

LINDA. *I* drank the wine.

BUD. (*Pulling out his lower lip.*) Oh, great. I'm getting a hive. Look at my lip. Look at my lip.

LINDA. But you didn't drink any wine.

BUD. Residue, Linda. Residue. Oh, listen, my chest is wheezing. (*BUD wheezes.*)

BUD. You hear that?

LINDA. I'm sorry, Bud. What can I do?

BUD. (*As HE wheezes, scratches and sneezes.*) Where are my Benadryl pills? I have to get some air. Here, open the windows, vacuum the dust, rinse out your mouth with alcohol, and shower with an unscented soap. I'll meet you in bed in forty-five minutes. (*HE sneezes again. Then poses romantically.*)

BUD. I want you.

LINDA. You're so romantic.

(*HE smiles. LIGHTS dim. SPOTLIGHT up on Sam.*)

SAM. When a couple first starts out, they try to look so attractive. She wears your favorite color. You wear cologne. You both keep in shape to be sexy. Well, guess what? That gets old really fast. Soon she's wearing whatever's clean, your cologne is three years old, and the only time you suck your stomach in, is when ex-girlfriends bump into you in a movie line. It's sad ... but the person you marry is not the person you end up with.

(*SPOTLIGHT out on Sam as LIGHTS come up on Mitchell and Fran coming home after a party, undressing for bed. MITCHELL now wears plaids with stripes, flood pants, and doesn't comb his hair. FRAN is fifty pounds heavier.*)

MITCHELL. Great party, huh?

FRAN. How would you know? You spent the whole night talking to that little tramp.

MITCHELL. She wasn't a little tramp. It was my boss's wife. We were just talking.

FRAN. About what? That little red leather mini-skirt she was wearing?

MITCHELL. Pink. It was a little pink leather mini-skirt. With twelve little buttons down the side.

FRAN. (*Walks away from Mitchell, undoing a scarf from her neck.*) I could wear one of those too, you know.

(*MITCHELL reacts with disgust.*)

FRAN. And I'd turn a helluva lot more heads.

(*MITCHELL mumbles something unflattering.*)

FRAN. What? You think I'm too fat, don't you?

MITCHELL. I didn't say that. I just don't think of you as the tight leather mini-skirt-type.

Remember last time you tried that? The noise it made when you walked down the street?

(*FRAN belches.*)

MITCHELL. Could you *please* cover your mouth when you do that?
FRAN. There's nobody here.

(*MITCHELL reacts. FRAN eats an apple.*)

FRAN. Besides, a good belch is the sign of a good meal.
MITCHELL. Then what is that noise you make all the time in the middle of the night? The sign of a good all you can eat banquet?
FRAN. You hate me cause I'm fat.
MITCHELL. I don't care what you weigh. All I'm saying ...
FRAN. Then you'll love me no matter big I get?
MITCHELL. Well, of ... How big were you thinking of getting?
FRAN. Well, let's face it. My mother is very heavy. And so is her mother and so was her mother. (*In baby talk.*) I'm afraid you'll hate me if I get that big and you'll leave me for some little skinny mini-skirted thing.
MITCHELL. That runs in your family? I thought your mother was, like, a medical oddity.

(*LIGHTS dim. SPOTLIGHT on Sam.*)

SAM. Every bad marriage has it's own sound. And if you listen very closely you'll hear the one sound they all have in common.

(LIGHTS up on Alan and Vickie in the midst of a heated argument.)

ALAN. The greatest astronaut of all times is Buzz Aldrin, I tell you!

VICKIE. Which just proves what an incredible imbecile you really are! Everyone knows the greatest astronaut of all times is Alan Shepherd!

ALAN. Alan Shepherd? Alan Shepherd? If that's what you think, you are the stupidest woman on the face of the earth!

VICKIE. And how would you know that? Do you *know* every stupid woman on the face of the earth?

ALAN. Maybe I do!

VICKIE. The only thing that qualifies me for being the stupidest woman on the face of the earth is the day I married you.

ALAN. Yeah? Well, you might as well know now, I only married you to get out of the army. That's how stupid I am. I could have stuck my head in underground tunnels looking for land mines, but, no, I had to marry you!

VICKIE. Is that so?

ALAN. Yes, that's so.

VICKIE. Then you're stupider than I even dreamed you could possibly be! The war had been over two years before we got married, you stupid idiot!

ALAN. Oh, Miss Current Events. I stand corrected. Now, you're an expert on the Army, are you?

VICKIE. What's it to you?

ALAN. (*"Mock" bowing in front of her.*) Oh, look at her. Miss Know-It-All. You were never even in the army.

VICKIE. Maybe I was.

ALAN. Oh, yeah? Well, then do you know who General Bradley was? Do you? Do you, you miserable woman? Do you even know who General Bradley was?

VICKIE. I don't have to answer that.

ALAN. You don't. Ha. I can't believe it. You don't even know who he was. That's how stupid you are! You don't even know who Momar Bradley was!

VICKIE. "Momar?" His name is "Omar." That makes you the stupidest man on the face of the planet, you incredibly stupid idiot. You are an incredibly stupid, stupid man.

ALAN. Then why don't you just drop dead?

VICKIE. After you!

ALAN. Don't tell *me* what to do!

VICKIE. I'll tell you anything I want. Drop Dead!

ALAN. Is that what you truly want? Is that what you truly want?

VICKIE. Yes. That's exactly what I want.

ALAN. Then just for spite, I'm not even going to drop dead! What do you think of that?

(*LIGHTS dim. SPOTLIGHT on Sam.*)

SAM. Every bad marriage has that sound. Oh, I'm not talking about the yelling. I'm talking about the sound of something "snapping." That one moment when something inside "snaps" and you say "What the hell am I doing married to this person?" Anything can trigger it. One of his bad jokes at a party. The way she hums while she cooks. The way he eats peanuts. And sometimes it's even more dramatic. "Snap."

(*SPOTLIGHT out on Sam. LIGHTS up on HAL as HE enters his bedroom, only to find RHONDA in bed with a nude man. There are three volumes of red books next to them.*)

HAL. Honey, I'm home!
RHONDA. (*Covering herself with a sheet.*) Early. You're home early. Are you trying to scare me to death?
HAL. No, but I ...

(*Underneath the sheets, a man's head pops up.*)

HAL. What's going on?
RHONDA. What do you mean?
HAL. There's a naked man underneath you.

(*The MAN lays back down.*)

RHONDA. Where?

HAL. There.

RHONDA. Oh, him?

HAL. Yes, him! Who is that?

RHONDA. Why?

HAL. "Why?" He's naked and you're in bed with him!

RHONDA. Can we discuss this later? I'm in the middle of something.

HAL. No, we can't discuss this later. Last week it was the newsboy. The week before that it was my Uncle Sid.

RHONDA. Please, Hal, not in front of the you-know-who. (*To Man.*) I'm sorry, he's not usually like this.

HAL. Who is he? Get off of him!

RHONDA. Questions. All these questions. We met this afternoon in the frozen food section at Foodtown. Happy?

HAL. Oh no. Not Jimmy the Stock Boy? I've done everything I can to please you. I hung upside down in space boots, I dressed up like a giant german shepherd, I painted my body with acrylic paint and learned to speak Spanish ...

RHONDA. What's your point, Hal?

HAL. How can you do this to me? Rhonda ... he's naked.

RHONDA. So?

HAL. So? He's in bed with you and he's naked!

RHONDA. Stop looking at him, Hal. Do you want people to think you're always looking at other men?

HAL. Of course not, but ...

RHONDA. I bet you don't even know what color my eyes are, anymore.

(*HAL'S face changes to a mixture of hatred and frustration. LIGHTS fade out. SPOTLIGHT up on Sam.*)

SAM. "Snap." But most of the time. It's something you should have seen coming all along.

(*SPOTLIGHT out on Sam as LIGHTS come up in the bedroom of Bud and Linda. SHE can no longer stand the sight of him.*)

BUD. Honey I'm home.

(*HE sneezes. SHE routinely blows his nose in a Kleenex. And spoons him some medicine.*)

LINDA. (*By rote.*) Your Metamucil.

(*HE drinks it.*)

LINDA. I went shopping today ...

BUD. Ssh. My sinuses are pounding. I swallowed mucous all day long. (*Gulps.*) There goes some more of it.

LINDA. (*Modeling her new outfit.*) Do you notice anything different?

BUD. Yes. I think I have a bunion on my left foot. It throbbed all morning. I think the hair on my foot is growing sideways because of it, too.

LINDA. (*By rote, and pretty well disgusted.*) Well, what would you like me to do?

BUD. You're not a doctor, Linda. I think I should see a doctor.

LINDA. I'll start the tub.

BUD. Linda ... please! Make sure the water is tepid. You know how hot water makes my hemorrhoids flare up.

LINDA. Do I.

BUD. You know, maybe I should just eat a little soup and go to bed.

LINDA. Fine. I'll go make you some soup.

BUD. You know, on second thought, I'm not even strong enough to eat. I have such problems with my stomach today. I flatulated all afternoon.

(*SHE exhales in exasperation.*)

BUD. Want to have sex?

(*On her look, the LIGHTS fade out. SPOTLIGHT on Sam.*)

SAM. "Snap." And when it comes, watch out. There's no turning back.

(SPOTLIGHT out on Sam, as LIGHTS come up in the bedroom of Mitchell and Fran. SHE is in bed. Another fifty pounds heavier. In a housecoat, eating ice cream out of the container in bed. Mallomars sit opened at her feet. SHE wears Jolene Bleach Creme on her "mustache." MITCHELL enters home from work. HE wears green pants and other ill-fitting colors. His hair looks even more unruly.)

MITCHELL. Honey, I'm home. *(HE reacts with disgust at the sight of the disgusting slob in the bed.)*

FRAN. Let's go, Mitchell. It's my fertile time. Chop. Chop.

MITCHELL. Now? I just walked in.

FRAN. Let's get shaking. I'm ovulating here.

MITCHELL. Aren't you going to brush your teeth and take your socks off?

FRAN. No. It's not your birthday, is it?

MITCHELL. Just thought I'd ask. *(HE starts to get undressed.)*

FRAN. Let's go. Let's go! I'm all heated up.

MITCHELL. Could you at least talk to me this time? It's hard to concentrate while you pick caramel out of your teeth.

FRAN. Just hand me those Mallomars, will you?

(HE does.)

FRAN. (*Chewing Mallomars.*) Now get in here and impregnate me. (*Baby talk.*) Your Couch Potato wants her Sweet Potato to make her Tater Tots.

MITCHELL. I wish I was dead.

FRAN. You're beginning to worry me, Mitchell. I'm starting to think you have another woman somewhere.

MITCHELL. Why would I look at other women when I know I've got you in my bed?

(*FRAN belches.*)

FRAN. (*Waving away the "belched air."*) Enchiladas. Let's go. Get those bony legs in here. What are you, a man or a mouse?

MITCHELL. Either way I sleep with a rodent.

FRAN. What did you say?

MITCHELL. I said we're out of deodorant.

FRAN. I never use it. It's bad for the environment.

MITCHELL. I don't feel very good.

FRAN. Come on. Make me feel like a woman.

(*FRAN belches silently, and pounds her chest. MITCHELL reacts with disgust. The LIGHTS dim. SPOTLIGHT on Sam.*)

SAM. "Snap." It's amazing what people will put up with, isn't it? It was at this point in these lovely marriages that I met up with these charming folks. I had just checked in to a little out of the way place called the Earle Brothers Honeymoon Lodge and Trout Fisharium, for a relaxing weekend of fishing and Stephen King novels.

(The Stage LIGHTS come up on the lodge. It is a rustic quaint New England Bed and Breakfast. Double-doors USR enter the old inn. A desk UC is filled with antiques. An archway stage R leads off to a dining room and library. Stairs stage L lead up to the bedrooms. The upstairs landing includes two practical guest room doors. There is a closet door DL.)

SAM. And now if you'll excuse me, I've got to check into the play. That's Pearl Earle, the innkeeper. She inherited this place from her father Earl Earle and his brother Burl.

(SAM goes to her. SHE wears historical New England dress and bonnet. His small suitcase and his Stephen King novel sit by the desk. HE is handed a key.)

PEARL. Well, now, you have yourself a nice quiet time, Mr. Crumm. And if there's anything I can do to make your stay more comfortable, you just let me know.

SAM. Thank you, Ma'am.

PEARL. My lending library is right off the dining room. Rowboats are out back and the woods are thick with venison.

SAM. Thanks again. (*To audience.*) And now, I'm going up to my room for some rest and relaxation. Don't worry. In about ten minutes you'll have an intermission to do the same thing.

(*SAM exits upstairs as ALAN and VICKIE enter UR and throw their suitcases on the floor one by one.*)

ALAN. Maybe if you'd learn how to read a map, we wouldn't have driven five miles out of the way.

VICKIE. Maybe if you read your own map before you left the house you'd know where the hell you were going.

ALAN. I knew where I was going

VICKIE. Then why did we have to ask that farmer where the hell we were?

ALAN. Because you made me turn left on Route 6 when I should have turned right.

VICKIE. Yeah. I made you turn left.

ALAN. Damn right! (*To Pearl.*) We have a reservation! Noah. Mr. and *Mrs.*

(*PEARL puts out a reservation book, and hands Alan a key.*)

VICKIE. You waited until we were in the middle of a five way intersection to throw that map in my face and start screaming: "Left turn or right turn?!" "Left turn or right turn?!"

ALAN. Right. Oh, yeah. Blame me. You make me sick to my stomach. You know that? Next time you drive.

VICKIE. That's fine with me, Mr. Senility. Mr. Leave-Your-Blinker-On. Twenty miles an hour in the passing lane with his blinker on for twenty-five minutes. Trucks were honking at you. People on foot were passing us, yelling things. It was humiliating.

ALAN. How would you even know what was going on? You spent every waking second changing the radio stations. How can you even hear what songs are playing before you push the button. Push the button. Push the button.

VICKIE. I need loud music blaring when I drive with you. I can't stand the sight of your miserable teeth-clenched face.

PEARL. Room Number Two. Top of the stairs. I gave you our nicest king-size bed.

ALAN. Oh, isn't this going to be the most fun vacation on earth.

VICKIE. Yeah. Maybe I'll get lucky and you'll swallow some fish hooks.

(VICKIE and ALAN exit to their room, as LINDA and BUD enter.)

PEARL. Welcome to the Earle Brothers Honeymoon Lodge and Trout Fisharium.

(BUD sneezes into the open reservation book. PEARL rips out the page and throws it away.)

LINDA. Stop it. Stop it. If you sneeze again, I'll knock your teeth down your throat.

BUD. There were horses in that field. I told you not to stop there.

LINDA. We were lost. If you hadn't been sneezing through that intersection, maybe we would have made the right turn.

BUD. (*Sing-song.*) Goldenrod. We parked by that field of goldenrod. My membranes are inflamed. Look. (*HE tries to show her his membranes.*)

LINDA.What choice did I have? I was not going to let you throw up on the upholstery again!

BUD.You know I get carsick. Who told you to leave the pail at home? (*To Pearl.*) I always get carsick. I always have. (*Re: Reservation book.*) Mr. and Mrs. Carmichael. Ever since I was a little sickly child, I got carsick. Usually I drive with my face covered in a handkerchief scented with Old Spice. It keeps me from getting nauseous.

(*TELEPHONE rings.*)

PEARL. Pardon me. (*Answers phone.*) Earle Brothers Honeymoon Lodge and Trout Fisharium. Pearl Earle speaking. Oh, hello Jeb. Yes, I got your flowers. Oh, Jeb! (*Giggles.*) I got guests, Jeb. Stop that, my ears are turning red.

BUD. Omigod. They are.

PEARL. (*Hangs up.*) Jeb Stuart. My beau. Well, now, you all make yourselves at home. The rowboats are by the lake. The woods are thick with venison. The reading library is just past the dining room. And you might enjoy our lovely grounds for a nice romantical walk about.

BUD. Linda, did you hear that? This place is a time bomb of disease and allergic reactions. The library is going to be filled with mold. The deer are probably filled with Lyme disease ridden ticks, and you know because of my colitis I can't get into a rowboat. I told you we should have gone to the Sterile Institute in St. Paul.

PEARL. Why exactly did you even come here?

LINDA. Solitude.

BUD. My nerves are bad and my heart needs a rest. Doctor's orders. My arteries are trying to strangle me.

(*HE holds out his arms to show her his arteries. LINDA imitates him behind his back.*)

PEARL. How nice for you. Shall I carry your bags up to your room?

LINDA. No. Thank you. We'll do it ourselves. Take the bags up to the room, Bud.

BUD. Without my truss?

LINDA. Just take them up to the room.

BUD. I'll pull myself.

PEARL. I'd be happy to oblige, ma'am.

LINDA. No, thank you. That's quite all right. Take the bags up to the room ... Bud.

BUD. All right. But you know about my problem. I hope nothing pops out of my canal. (*HE exits upstairs with the suitcases.*)

LINDA. Miss Earle, did you set up our room just the way I asked you to?

PEARL. Yes, Ma'am. Fresh cut flowers. Horse hair blankets. Goose down pillows. Flannel sheets. Lots of antiques. And I let the cat run around in there all afternoon.

LINDA. (*Tips her.*) Thank you. It's our second honeymoon. And I want everything to be just perfect.

(*BUD starts sneezing like a maniac offstage as LINDA laughs deviously and exits. FRAN enters the front door. SHE wears overalls and looks like Porky Pig. SHE has gained another fifty pounds. SHE has ice cream stains on her shirt and mouth. A beige coat is draped over her arm.*)

FRAN. Hurry up, Mitchell! Get the lead out! I want to eat lunch!

(*MITCHELL enters in a red checked hunting jacket and a big fur "Elmer Fudd" hat with two ear flaps that stick out on the sides. HE carries in their suitcases and has a double-barrel shotgun on his shoulder.*)

PEARL. Don't tell me. Mrs. and Mr. Bush?

FRAN. Yeah. What's it to you, Dolly Madison?

MITCHELL. What do you have in this thing, concrete? It weighs a ton.

FRAN. Cheddar Cheese. (*To Pearl.*) I like to snack when I'm in bed.

PEARL. I never would've guessed.

MITCHELL. (*Muttering to himself.*) Just once I'd like to make love to a woman who isn't covered in crumbs ... and lint ...

FRAN. What are you saying?

MITCHELL. I said I hoped you packed your Tums and mints.

PEARL. Room Number One. Top of the stairs. I see you brought your hunting gear, Mr. Bush.

MITCHELL. Yeah. I'm dying to get out there and mow down a few moose.

FRAN. Good thing we stopped to ask that farmer directions. What a great produce stand. These tomatoes are so juicy. (*SHE bites into a tomato and juice gushes all over her face.*)

FRAN. I could eat the whole bushel. Hey, Martha Washington, we all checked in yet? I want to get out of these clothes. My pants are riding up to China.

MITCHELL. Let's hurry. We want to get out and hunt those moose, don't we?

FRAN. I'm going as fast as I can. Are you sure this coat you gave me is for moose hunting? It weighs a ton.

MITCHELL. Well it wouldn't if you'd take the salami out of the pockets. Now, do you remember what to do when you actually see a moose?

FRAN. What am I, an idiot? Of course I remember. I hold two sticks over my head like this and make the moose call. That's the signal. You think I'm really stupid, don't you?

MITCHELL. No, I don't. You want to try it once?

FRAN. I can remember a moose signal, Mitchell. (*SHE mimes holding sticks over her head. SHE makes moose noises.*) How's that?

MITCHELL. (*Grinning.*) That'll be just fine.

(*SHE exits upstairs. HE follows pointing his rifle at her back. HAL and RHONDA enter with their suitcases.*)

HAL. (*To Rhonda.*) How did that farmer know your name? We never met that guy.

RHONDA. I don't know. Oh, yes. I used to come up here when I was a kid.

HAL. You never did. You grew up in Florida.

RHONDA. So what? He guessed my name. A lot of farmers can do that.

HAL. Forget it. Never mind. Let's just check in. I want to get out of these clothes.

RHONDA. Oh, good. What costumes did you bring?

HAL. None. Listen, Rhonda. I'm sick of dressing up to have sex. Can't we just have sex like we used to? You know, you and me? Naked?

RHONDA. What for?

HAL. "What for?!"

RHONDA. I asked you first.

HAL. All right. Skip it. You win. I'll put an ice bucket on my head and pretend I'm "The Man in The Golden Helmet." Okay?

RHONDA. Ooh. That's my favorite. Can I call you other people's names?

HAL. Fine.

(*RHONDA checks in.*)

PEARL. Wheeler?

RHONDA. That's us. Hal and Rhonda Wheeler. Say, what a lovely, pure, chaste and unsullied pilgrim costume you're wearing.

HAL. (*HE walks away DL. To himself.*) This is going to be the best night I ever spent. (*HE packs his pistol in his jacket pocket.*)

(*ALAN and VICKIE enter from upstairs. With fishing rods and a picnic basket.*)

VICKIE. Would you mind waiting up for me? We're not in Japan, you know.

ALAN. Yeah? Well, we're not snails either. Come on. Let's go. I want to go and fish.

VICKIE. What you want to do is go and drink beer while I row you around the lake.

ALAN. Oh, thank you. Now I have a translator.

(THEY exit. We see VICKIE has a power hand drill—the kind for poking holes in boats. SHE revs it as SHE exits. MITCHELL enters from upstairs with his rifle. HAL approaches him.)

HAL. Pfft. Pfft.

(MITCHELL waves away an imaginary fly.)

HAL. Pfft!!
MITCHELL. Are you pffting me?
HAL. Want to sleep with my wife?
MITCHELL. What?
HAL. My wife has been eying you since we came in, and I was wondering if you'd be willing to sleep with her.
MITCHELL. What?
HAL. I said my wife has been eying you since we came in.

(MITCHELL looks over at the wife.)

PEARL. Well, ma'am. There's a burly mailman who comes by every other morning ...
MITCHELL. She's beautiful.
HAL. Yeah, I know.
MITCHELL. You're asking me to sleep with your own wife?
HAL. Yes. You see, I uh ... suffered a war wound. In 'Nam.
MITCHELL. Viet Nam.

HAL. No, Namtucket. I was spinnaker flying and I landed on a buoy the wrong way. Anyway, it's a long story and please don't make me relive that hell again.

MITCHELL. No, of course not.

HAL. And now, the only way I can satisfy my wife is to offer her other men.

MITCHELL. (*Grinning, as HE eyes Rhonda.*) That's horrible.

HAL. Yes, it is. But if you do this, I think all my problems will soon be over. (*HE pats his pistol.*)

MITCHELL. Really?

HAL. Yeah, there's something about this place that just makes me feel lucky.

MITCHELL. (*Pats his rifle.*) Yeah? I feel the same way myself.

FRAN. (*Reappears from upstairs.*) Let's go kill something, Mitchell!

HAL. What is that?

MITCHELL. That's *my* wife.

HAL. Oh. (*To Fran.*) Nice to meet you.

FRAN. (*Belches in Hal's face.*) Corndog.

(*SHE waves away the "belched air." HAL joins her in fanning it away.*)

HAL. (*To Mitchell, sotto.*) Listen, if you change your mind, put an ice bucket on your head and come up to our room.

MITCHELL. Right. Well, let's go, Fran.

FRAN. Like this, right? (*Holds sticks over her head and gives the moose call.*)

MITCHELL. Excellent. If I didn't know you were my wife, I'd think you were a real live moose.

(*FRAN exits. We see a huge bull's-eye embossed on the back of her jacket. MITCHELL aims his rifle and exits after her.*)

End of Act I

ACT II

Scene 1

(*The Lodge. Later that day. SAM enters from outside with a fishing rod.*)

SAM. In the fifteen minutes you've been gone, four hours have passed. I've been out fishing all afternoon. Caught three trout. But I threw them all back. In fact, I don't even know why I go fishing. It's sort of like doing nothing, except you have to hold on to something while you're doing it. And now, if you'll excuse me, I have to start my book.

(*HAL enters from upstairs as SAM heads for the dining room.*)

HAL. Pfft. Pfft. Pfft.

(*SAM swats a snat and exits. HAL looks around. HE takes out his pistol and enacts his "murder scheme."*)

HAL. (*Surprising another man with his wife.*) Oh, sleep with my wife, will you? Take this! Bam! Whoops, I slipped. Honey ... are you all right? What? You're dead? Gee, what a terrible shame. Bam!

(*HE giggles to himself as PEARL enters.*)

PEARL. What's so funny?
HAL. Oh, I was thinking about that joke about the two Irishmen.
PEARL. Oh, yes.

(*SHE laughs like a loon. HAL backs away. ALAN and VICKIE enter. They're soaking wet.*)

ALAN. Hey, Pearl, I think there's something wrong with your boat.
PEARL. My boat?
ALAN. No, the Queen Mary. Look at me.
PEARL. Well, what on earth did you do, tip the boat over?
ALAN. No, we didn't tip the boat "ovah"! It sank! It was full of holes!
VICKIE. He almost drowned. Almost. Somehow our picnic basket got tangled on Alan's feet and when the boat went down, he sank like a cement block. I swam to shore and tried calling for help. But my voice is so weak.
ALAN. Luckily the lake was only four feet deep.
VICKIE. You really should post signs. It looks a lot deeper than it is!
ALAN. I have sand in my pants.

VICKIE. Now I'm going to have to think of something else.

ALAN. For what?

VICKIE. For us. This is our second honeymoon. That is, if you count the first one.

PEARL. I'll be right back. You go warm yourselves up, I'll make you some of my famous cocoa. (*Exits.*)

ALAN. You always have to bring that up, don't you? (*To Hal.*) I forgot to make reservations for our honeymoon and she acts like it was the end of the world.

VICKIE. We spent the night in a pup tent, behind a rest stop on the Jersey Turnpike. (*SHE wraps a blanket around her shoulders and exits to her room.*)

ALAN. Ooh. I should have backed the car over her when I had the chance.

HAL. Pfft.

(*ALAN swats a gnat.*)

HAL. Pfft.

(*ALAN slaps the back of his neck.*)

HAL. Hey. I'm pffting here.

ALAN. Oh, sorry. What can I do for you?

HAL. Want to sleep with my wife?

ALAN. What?

HAL. Look, I've got an embarrassing wound and I'm forced to supply my wife with an endless stream of men. Okay? Now, do you want to sleep with my wife or not? I'm on a schedule.

(*RHONDA appears on the landing. SHE is dressed in a sexy nightgown and a plumed helmet.*)

RHONDA. Hal! I've been waiting. Exactly when does the Ice Bucket Man Cometh?
HAL. I'll be right up, my dear.

(*SHE exits.*)

ALAN. Is that?
HAL. Yes.
ALAN. And you want me to...
HAL. Yes.
ALAN. With her?
HAL. Yes.
ALAN. Yes? Okay!

(*ALAN starts up the stairs. FRAN enters from outside and rings the desk bell.*)

HAL. Wait. Uh ... Not now. When there are less people around.
ALAN. I'll shut the door.
HAL. Look. It's bad enough a stranger's gonna do this with my wife. But I don't have to stand here and let people watch me be humiliated like this, do I?
ALAN. I guess not.

HAL Okay. At midnight, come to our room, knock three times and say, "Fear not, Helpless Female Ranch Owner. It is I." Then my wife will open the door, you take her to the bed. Ravish her. And it'll be fireworks all over.

ALAN. If you insist.

(HAL hands him a Lone Ranger/burglar mask.)

HAL. Here.
ALAN. What is this?
HAL. A mask.
ALAN. I have to wear a mask?
HAL. It helps my wife remember me.

(ALAN nods and exits. FRAN is at desk, ringing the bell again.)

FRAN. *(Calling for Pearl.)* Hey, Wax Ears! I'm ringing a bell here, for God's Sake.
PEARL. *(Off.)* Coming!

(HAL takes ice bucket off front desk.)

FRAN. What is she, dead back there?
HAL. Who?
FRAN. "Who?" Mind your own beeswax, chucklehead.

(HAL exits upstairs as PEARL enters from the back.)

PEARL. (*To Fran.*) Sorry. I was baking a little Apple Brown Betty. And my cocoa boiled over. You rang the bell?

FRAN. Good guess, Betsy Ross. There's been a terrible accident. My husband's been shot.

PEARL. Where?

FRAN. Right in the ass. He sat on his gun. The stupid moron.

PEARL. Where is he now?

FRAN. He's out in the woods, sitting in a pile of leaves, trying to clot the flow.

PEARL. Oh, dear!

(*PEARL takes out a first aid kit, as SHE and FRAN run out the door. SAM enters from the dining room, eating a banana.*)

SAM. I love the country. No matter where you look, there is great beauty.

(*LINDA enters from upstairs in a negligee.*)

SAM. And here comes some more of it.

LINDA. Where is she? Pearl? Miss Earle!

SAM. I think she's outside. Is something wrong?

LINDA. It's my husband!

SAM. What's wrong with him?

LINDA. Nothing. And that's what's wrong.

BUD. (*Appears on the landing.*) Linda, come back to bed. I've got my mesh bikini pants on.

(BUD exits. LINDA starts to scratch.)

LINDA. Did you see that?

SAM. Not really. His robe was closed.

LINDA. When we walked in here, he was allergic to everything. Weeds. Sheets. The color orange. After what he's been through he should have swelled up and choked to death. And now, look at him!

SAM. It's a miracle. *(HE picks up the banana peel he dropped.)* Whoops. Be careful. I wouldn't want anyone to slip and break their neck.

LINDA. God, I didn't even see that. *(Then.)* "Break their neck?" *(Looks upstairs and laughs.)* Where did you get that?

SAM. In the dining room. There's a whole bunch of them.

LINDA. Good. I love a nice midnight snack. *(Laughs.)* Thank you. Thank you. Thank you. *(SHE kisses him and exits upstairs.)*

SAM. *(To audience.)* Women are usually grateful for a fine piece of fruit.

(A MAN in a Revolutionary War outfit enters. It is JEB STUART.)

JEB. Hello. I'm Jeb Stuart.

SAM. Jeb Stuart. Really? I thought you were in the *Civil* War.

JEB. No, no. I'm Pearl Earle's beau. Jeb Stuart. Owner of the Drum and Musket Family Style Restaurant, out on Route 14.

(*ALAN enters from his room. VICKIE follows.*)

ALAN. Oh, get a load of the Y-O-K-E-L.

(*MITCHELL is carried in by FRAN and PEARL.*)

MITCHELL. Oh. Oh. Oh ...
ALAN. What happened to you?
PEARL. He shot off a good portion of his buttocks.
MITCHELL. (*Sees Jeb and Pearl.*) Oh, I think I have a fever. What year is it?

(*MITCHELL stares at Jeb and Pearl. THEY look at each other and shrug. SAM takes the shotgun.*)

PEARL. We should get him up into bed.
SAM. Here, let me take that shotgun, fella.
MITCHELL. No. No. Please. I was so close. My hand just slipped. Please let me go back out there. Two years of planning down the drain. Two years of planning and waiting and hoping ...
FRAN. Later. We'll go out again later, Mitchell.
MITCHELL. Later? Yeah. Like when there are less people around. Like ... midnight. Sure. Midnight is the best time to hunt moose. You sneak up on them while they're sleeping and Blam! Blam! Blam! Moosemeat.

FRAN. Fine. We'll go at midnight. Now get up to bed. (*Babytalk.*) I'm feewing fwisky and want Papa Bear to see who's been sweeping in her bed.

(*MITCHELL is dragged off to his room by FRAN and SAM.*)

MITCHELL. I want to hunt. I want to hunt. I have to hunt.

ALAN. I think the guy wants to hunt.

PEARL. Men like their bloodsports. Like Jeb, here.

JEB. Yup. I like shooting bats.

VICKIE. Really?

JEB. Pearl's got a whole slew of them out back up past them oaks. We often spend our evenings staring at the stars and blowing bats brains out with my beebee gun.

PEARL. Remember last year when we had one in the inn.

JEB. Yup. A big old bat got loose in here. We found him up in that room there.

ALAN. That's our room.

PEARL. Jeb had to smash his brains in.

JEB. With a baseball bat. I'm on a semi-pro team.

PEARL. Now I keep a baseball bat right there in that closet.

VICKIE. You don't say. Had to beat it to death with a baseball bat, huh?

PEARL. Just about ruined my little flowered wallpaper too.

ALAN. Oh, is that what that is. I thought every room came with its own Rorschach test.

JEB. I'd do anything to protect my Pearl.

PEARL. Oh, now you stop it, Jeb. My ears are turning red.

ALAN. My God. They are.

VICKIE. Gee, it would be terrible if another bat got in here and you had to beat its brains in with a baseball bat. Especially if it landed on somebody's head first.

ALAN. No kidding.

(ALAN and VICKIE exit to the dining room.)

PEARL. Jeb, what on earth are you doing here? You should be outside your steakhouse sitting on your cannon.

JEB. Had to see your pretty face.

PEARL. Oh, Jeb.

JEB. Pearl Earle, I'm your man, like it or not. I live, eat and breathe for you I'm so full of love. You're my every thought. My every desire. My every breath.

(ALAN and VICKIE enter from the dining room.)

JEB. My life is meaningless without you.

ALAN. You think your life is meaningless now? Wait until you're married a few years. Then you'll see just how meaningless life can be, you stupid rube.

(On their looks, we:)

BLACKOUT

ACT II

Scene 2

(Midnight CHIMES from a grandfather clock. MOONLIGHT spills in the quiet lobby. SAM enters from upstairs with his book, in his pajamas, robe and slippers.)

SAM. It's cold in here, isn't it? Hey, don't make fun of my pajamas. Normally I sleep in the nude, but I don't know most of you people. So I thought I'd put something on. And now, if you'll excuse me. I'm going to get a nice warm glass of milk.

(SAM exits to the dining room. VICKIE enters from upstairs. SHE peeks to make sure Alan is asleep. SHE quietly closes the door and tiptoes down the steps. SHE looks around, opens the closet door. A hard wooden baseball bat falls to the floor. VICKIE quietly picks it up and restores it in the closet. SHE takes out a

*butterfly net and exits outside. LINDA tiptoes
downstairs, itching and scratching. SHE
laughs, wheezes, and exits to the kitchen. JEB
enters in a courting suit. With a corsage. HE
rings the desk bell and kneels. When there is
no answer:)*

JEB. All right. I'll just go back to my truck, get
a ladder and ask her proper. From right outside
her bedroom window.

*(JEB exits as HAL enters from his room. HE
wears a Lone Ranger mask.)*

HAL. Be right back, Helpless Female Ranch
Owner.

*(HAL sneaks down the steps and takes off his
mask. HE pulls out his gun from his bathrobe
pocket and rehearses whipping it out. HE isn't
very good. HE drops bullets all over the floor.
HE quickly gathers his bullets as ALAN enters
in his pajamas and burglar mask. HE taps Hal
on the shoulder which scares him. HE gives
Hal the "thumbs up" and peeks out from under
his mask so Hal will know it is him. HAL
gives the "thumbs up" back, and hides as
ALAN tiptoes to Hal's room and knocks on the
door. His bathrobe is similar to Hal's.)*

ALAN. Fear not, Helpless Female Ranch
Owner. It is me!

HAL. I!
RHONDA. (*Opens the door. SHE wears a cowboy hat and a holster.*) O Masked Man! How can I repay you?

(*RHONDA pulls Alan into her room. HE gives a "thumbs up" to Hal as HE is dragged off. SHE closes the door. HAL packs his gun. HE counts to ten and gleefully gets ready to kill his wife.*)

HAL. (*To Rhonda.*) And now, you're gonna get yours.

(*HAL whips out his gun again. The bullets fly all over again. HE quickly gathers them up. LINDA enters from the dining room. SHE carries bananas, which SHE is peeling and eating. SHE scares Hal.*)

HAL. Ah!
LINDA. What are you doing?
HAL. Sleepwalking.
LINDA. But you're awake.
HAL. I know. I have insomnia. (*HE notices the banana.*)
LINDA. (*Guilty.*) It's for my husband.
HAL. Oh, you too, huh?

(*LINDA exits upstairs.*)

HAL. (*To Rhonda.*) And now you're gonna get yours.

(*Before Hal can get upstairs, MITCHELL limps down from his room, in his hunting gear and hunting hat, with his shotgun and a bear trap. His ass is in a sling. HAL hides until HE exits outside. MITCHELL is still in a lot of pain.*)

MITCHELL. Ooh. Ooh. Oooh.
HAL. (*To Rhonda, starting to get nervous.*) And now you're gonna get yours ...

(*HAL starts up the stairs, but LINDA reenters blocking his way. SHE is scratching and itching. Peels hang out of her pockets.*)

LINDA. You're still here?
HAL. Huh? Yeah.
LINDA. Have you tried counting sheep?
HAL. No, but I dressed up like one last Saturday.
LINDA. Oh. Well. Uh ... my husband needs more bananas.
HAL. How proud you must be.

(*LINDA exits to the dining room, scratching and sneezing.*)

HAL. (*To Rhonda, very nervous.*) And now you're gonna get yours!

(FRAN enters blocking his way. SHE wears her moose hunting coat.)

FRAN. Do you mind? I'm walking here!
HAL. I have to...
FRAN. I said "I am walking here."
HAL. I know, but I ...
FRAN. Are you going to back up or am I going to step on your face?
RHONDA. *(Off.)* Oh, Ranger!
HAL. *(Looks at his watch.)* But I ...

(SHE barrels down the steps. HE jumps to get out of her way.)

FRAN. Have you seen my husband? We're supposed to go midnight moose hunting. And if he left without me, I'll crack his neck like a chicken bone.

(LINDA enters from the kitchen eating a banana.)

HAL. No, I ...
FRAN. *(To Linda.)* Hey, where'd you get those bananas?
LINDA. In the dining room.
FRAN. I could use a little snack. This country air gives me an appetite. Show me where!

(FRAN dumps her moose coat on the deacon's bench and exits with Linda. HAL is starting to sweat.)

HAL. (*To Rhonda.*) And now you'll finally get yours!

(*HAL goes to door. We hear "Oh Masked Man!" "Oh Masked Man!" ALAN is making horse noises. HAL goes to open the door as he rehearsed, but the door is locked from inside. HE checks for his key. We hear more "Oh Masked Man." "And Tonto too." "Circle the wagons."*)

HAL. Where are my keys? Oh God, where are my keys! (*HE knocks on door.*) Pfft. Pfft! (*HE slaps the back of his own neck.*) Open up. Hello. Hello! Stop it. That's enough now. Room service. Hello! (*HE pulls out gun to shoot doorknob off. The bullets all fall out on the floor. HE panics.*)

ALAN. (*Off.*) Hiyo Silver....

(*HAL reacts in horror.*)

ALAN. (*Off.*) Away!!
HAL. Go through the window! A ladder. Get a ladder! And go through the window!

(*HE exits outside, as VICKIE enters from outside with a live bat in her butterfly net. SHE tiptoes upstairs and opens her room, letting the bat free in her room. SHE closes the door quickly, then sneaks down to the bottom of the stairs, and opens the closet. The baseball bat falls to the floor. SHE picks it up and gets inside the closet. SAM enters with LINDA from the dining room.)*

SAM. *(To Linda.)* It's cold in here. Isn't it cold in here to you?
LINDA. Here. Put this on!

(SAM puts on Fran's coat.)

LINDA. And go to bed.

(MITCHELL starts to enter and sees his wife's coat. HE giggles, takes his gun and exits outside to get ready.)

LINDA. *(Shoving Sam upstairs.)* Goodnight!
SAM. Goodnight.

(LINDA pushes Sam down the hall. Now the coast is clear and LINDA starts peeling bananas frantically. Outside the front door, HAL runs by, a raving lunatic.)

HAL. A ladder. Somebody get me a ladder.

(LINDA starts peeling bananas and dropping the peels on the stairs, eating them as SHE does it. A whole cluster of peels are pulled from her pockets. SHE covers the staircase with them.

*Behind her, outside the front doors, JEB sets
up a ladder and calls up.)*

JEB. I'm not waiting any longer, Pearl Earle. I
won't spend another day on this planet without
you by my side. I love you, Pearl Earle, and I
want you to be mine.
PEARL. (*Off.*) Oh, Jeb!
JEB. Will you marry me?
PEARL. (*Off.*) Yes, Jeb, yes.
JEB. Yahoo! Hang on. I'm coming up. We're
eloping.
PEARL. (*Off.*) Oh, Jeb, my ears are turning
red.
JEB. Omigod, they are.

(*JEB climbs up out of sight. LINDA continues to
scratch and sneeze. Once the stairs are covered
with bananas, SHE calls out.*)

LINDA. Bud! Oh, Bud, darling! Could you
come down here for a minute?
SAM. (*Reenters.*) Left my book in the kitchen.
(*HE goes to step down the stairs.*)
LINDA. No!!
RHONDA. (*Off. Halting him in his tracks.*)
No!
SAM. (*Stopping.*) Sure I did.
RHONDA (*Off.*) Stop. Don't move!

(*SAM stops.*)

RHONDA. (*Off.*) Oh, stop! Help me. I'm so helpless. No, no, don't take my land!

SAM. (*Reacts.*) Who is that?

RHONDA. (*Off.*) No, no, don't fence me in!

SAM. (*Banging on the door.*) Are you all right in there?

ALAN. (*Off.*) Go away!

RHONDA. (*Off.*) Somebody save me! Who are you, Masked Man?

SAM. Hey, what's going on in there?

ALAN. (*Off.*) Get lost!

SAM. You hear that?

LINDA. (*Scratching like a dog against the desk.*) Yes. Go back to bed.

RHONDA. (*Off.*) Oh no! Not the corral!

SAM. Oh no! Not the corral! (*He tries the door. It's locked.*) Don't worry, lady. I'll save you. Adjoining room! Go through the adjoining room!

(*SAM steps into the next room. HE shuts the door. HE screams a BLOOD-CURDLING SCREAM. The door flies open and SAM is fighting off a bat which is imbedded in his hair. LINDA screams. SAM continues screaming and dashes to the stairs, where HE slips on banana peels and slips down the steps. BUD, RHONDA and ALAN appear as the commotion gets wild.*)

LINDA. A bat! He has a bat in his hair!

(*VICKIE steps out and bashes Sam's brains in.
PEOPLE scream. SAM stumbles forward as
FRAN enters from the dining room eating
pretzel sticks and belches in his face. PEOPLE
scream again. HAL enters with a ladder which
cracks off rung by rung as HE runs it through
Sam's neck. SAM screams again, spitting out
teeth. SAM staggers out the front door. We
hear the BEAR TRAP SHUT on his foot. HE
stumbles onstage screaming and swatting the
bat, bruised and battered, his leg in the trap.
PEOPLE still scream. SAM staggers back out
the door and we hear two loud GUNSHOTS.
HE crumbles to the floor. From above him, we
hear:*)

JEB and PEARL. (*Off.*) Oh, Jeb!!! The
ladder!!!

(*TWO BODIES [Jeb and Pearl] plummet to their
deaths crushing Sam. As the dust settles on
poor Sam, EVERYONE reacts in horror.*)

ALL. Ooh. (*ALL face out front in shock.*)

BLACKOUT

ACT II

Scene 3

(SAM is DC in his SPOTLIGHT. The OTHERS are frozen in place.)

SAM. Maybe now you'll understand why I'm so bitter. Thanks to these four couples I lost three toes, seven teeth, my thumb, broke my spine and got this metal plate in my head. What came next? Well, I'm sure you have your own ideas. For you happy ending purists, it could have ended something like this:

("HAPPY MUSIC" plays as SAM "rewinds" himself, walking "backwards" into position to be shot all over again. Two GUNSHOTS go off and HE falls to the ground. The BODIES of Jeb and Pearl plummet to their deaths with "Oh, Jebbb!!!" "The ladder!!!" Everyone "Oohs.")

MITCHELL. Are you all right?

(SAM, JEB and PEARL enter, unscathed.)

SAM. I'm fine. This thick coat stopped the bullets. And nothing else hurt me much, because luckily, I work out.

ALL. Aah.

PEARL. Are you all right, Jeb?

JEB. Luckily we landed on our heads. It's a miracle!

ALL. Ooh.

PEARL. And now we're free to get married and spend the rest of our lives together in eternal bliss.

JEB. Am I the luckiest man on the planet or what?

(THEY giggle and exit together. All ad-lib "munchkin-like" goodbyes.)

FRAN. Omigod, Mitchell. That could have been me.

MITCHELL. Thank God, you're all right. What was I thinking?

FRAN. It's all right, Mitchell. I'm still here.

(THEY pose head to head, smiling out front.)

ALL. Ah.

HAL. Boy, what a close call.

RHONDA. Hal? *(To Alan.)* Who are you?

ALAN. *(Confused.)* The Lone Ranger?

(RHONDA slaps him. HE wake sup.)

VICKIE. Alan? What are you doing?

ALAN. Sleepwalking! Believe me, I didn't know what I was doing.

RHONDA. It's true. He really didn't. (*RHONDA goes to Hal.*) Oh, honey. I thought he was you.

HAL. Really?

RHONDA. Only not as good. Oh, Hal. All this time, whenever I slept with other men it was only because I was thinking of you.

(*ALL smile and nod.*)

RHONDA. And now, I know that I was wrong. Now I know what I really want more than anything is to spend eternity sleeping with you ... and thinking of them.

(*ALL smile and nod.*)

HAL. Do you really mean it?

RHONDA. You know I do.

ALL. Ah.

HAL. You've made me very happy, Rhonda. Almost as happy as ... the plant lady and the janitor.

(*ALL titter like women into their hands. HAL and RHONDA giggle and run off. ALL ad-lib "goodnights."*)

BUD. Linda, are you all right?

LINDA. (*Wheezing.*) Oh, Bud ... I've been such a fool. Don't ever leave me.

BUD. After all these years together? Don't even think of it.

LINDA. But I'm such a mess.

BUD. Not to me. You're my own little bundle of hives. And I'm Mr. Back Scratcher.

(*ALL smile and nod.*)

LINDA. Do you mean it?

BUD. Do I! Now it's my turn to take care of you.

ALL. Ah.

BUD. Let's go cover each other in Calamine Lotion.

(*ALL titter like women into their hands.*)

LINDA. Oh, you're so good to me.

(*THEY giggle and exit. ALL ad-lib "goodnights."*)

ALAN. Sure makes our problems seem so ... stupid.

VICKIE. Oh, Alan. You're so right. And you always were.

ALAN. Guess what? Today is the eight year two month anniversary of our first kiss. And to celebrate, I booked us into our own private suites at all of Europe's top hotels.

ALL. Ooh.

ALAN. If we leave right now we can just make the plane!

VICKIE. Wait. Don't you need your map?

ALAN. Are you kidding? I memorized the route.

(ALAN and VICKIE giggle and exit. ALL ad-lib "goodbyes.")

FRAN. Ain't love grand? It makes life worth living.

MITCHELL. Don't I know it. My wittle sweet potato.

FRAN. Uh-uh-uh. Mitchell. Fwom now on I'm gonna be your skinny wittle fwench fwy.

(THEY giggle and exit. Ad-lib "goodbyes." After they exit, and a silence has taken over the stage:)

SAM. Too bad that's *not* how things ended. For all you dark-sided cynics, like me, there's this delightful conclusion.

(Dark scary MUSIC plays as SAM once again gets blown away by the SHOTGUN. This time, however, JEB and PEARL don't fall. Then:)

FRAN. Omigod, Mitchell. That could have been me.

MITCHELL. (*Crying.*) I know.
FRAN. Don't cry, Mitchell. I'm still here.

(*MITCHELL: undistinguishable sobs.*)

RHONDA. Hal? (*To Alan.*) Who are you?
ALAN. The Lone Ranger.

(*RHONDA slaps him hard.*)

VICKIE. Alan? What are you doing?

(*VICKIE slaps him harder as RHONDA goes to Hal.*)

RHONDA. Oh, Hal. I only did this because I loved you.
HAL. That's okay. It's part of who you are. Hey, guess what? Today is Saturday. So it's my turn to pick. Let's go play Eva and The Fuhrer.
RHONDA. We never played that before ...
HAL. Quick Eva, to the Bunker!

(*HAL draws his pistol as THEY exit to their room. We hear a GUNSHOT. RHONDA is shot dead and falls into the lobby. Another GUNSHOT. HAL enters, dead, falls over the railing. LINDA wheezes uncontrollably.*)

BUD. Linda, are you all right?
LINDA. (*Clutching at her asthma-racked throat.*) I can't breathe. I can't breathe. I ....

(SHE falls to the floor, wheezing and choking. Commotion. SHE twitches and dies.)

FRAN. Omigod ... She's dead.

BUD. Yes! I mean ... Poor Linda .... *(HE grins.)*

MITCHELL. Ooh. You lucky dog.

FRAN. What did you say?

MITCHELL. I said I have a little frog.

VICKIE. Shouldn't we call somebody?

ALAN. Who? Sam Peckinpaw? They're dropping like flies around here. Let's get out of here.

(ALAN and VICKIE run out and get in their car.)

BUD. Well, there's really no point in staying anymore. My wife's dead, we're out of food ... *(HE heads for his room. HE stops when he hears:)*

VICKIE. *(Off.)* Read your *own* map!

ALAN. *(Off.)* Get that map out of my face!!

(FRAN looks outside as Alan and Vickie's car crashes horribly into a tree.)

(SFX: AGONIZING CAR WRECK and SCREAMS A HUB CAP rolls onstage..)

FRAN. Omigod. They're dead.

(MITCHELL goes to shoot her with shotgun, it jams twice. HE turns it around to fix it and the gun goes off blowing BUD away. FRAN gobbles pretzel sticks.)

FRAN. Look what you did, Mitchell. Look what you did. *(SHE chokes and gags on her pretzel sticks and dies, coughing and spitting.)*
MITCHELL. *(Looks around. The last survivor.)* Well, no use me sticking around.

(MITCHELL steps out the front door. We hear: "Oh, Jeeebbbb..." As JEB and PEARL fall on him and kill him. LIGHTS fade. LIGHTS come back up on Sam Crumm, DC, in his SPOTLIGHT.)

SAM. But life is never black and white. No happy endings and no blood baths. This is what really happened: Soon after Jeb and Pearl plummeted to their deaths...
JEB and PEARL. *(Off.)* Oh Jeb! The ladder!

(SOUND of bodies splatting on the ground.)

SAM. ... Mitchell and Hal were arrested and charged with a conspiracy killing.

(LIGHTS up DR on HAL and MITCHELL frozen with fear. THEY wear numbers, HAL—a hairnet, and MITCHELL—a bandana.)

SAM. They are currently spending the rest of their lives on death row. Cellmates, craft partners. And love slaves to a Chicano gang.

MITCHELL. (*To Hal.*) It's your turn.

HAL. (*To Mitchell.*) No, it's your turn.

MITCHELL. (*To Hal.*) No, it's your turn.

HAL. (*To Mitchell.*) No, it's your turn.

MITCHELL. No, it's Saturday.

(*HAL's eyes bug out in fear as the LIGHTS fade out.*)

SAM. Fran divorced Mitchell and started on a mad eating binge. She was recently arrested for attempting to wash herself publicly at a local Suds 'N Soap Auto Care Center.

(*LIGHTS up DL on FRAN, a thousand pound grotesque naked fat woman, holding a towel over herself in one hand and a soapy sponge in the other.*)

FRAN. Hey, Rag Boy! Hand me that Windex! Hey, hey! What are you looking at? What the hell are you looking at?

(*LIGHTS fade out.*)

SAM. Rhonda had to learn to slow down a little. Nine months after this story took place, she gave birth. To twins.

(*LIGHTS up DL on RHONDA, who holds two babies. One wears a plumed helmet, the other a Lone Ranger mask.*)

RHONDA. (*Proudly.*) They're just like their fathers.

(*LIGHTS fade out.*)

SAM. Linda left Bud and moved to the Village. She never thought of marriage or men the same way again.

(*LINDA appears DR dressed in black leather and chains, with a Storm Trooper helmet and knee-high boots. SHE drags on a cigarette butt.*)

LINDA. (*To offstage character DC.*) I told you to lick my boots, Helen. You know what happens to "Naughty Girls." (*To Sam.*) What? You got a problem?
SAM. No. Nice hat.

(*LIGHTS fade out.*)

SAM. Bud gave up his legal career and went in search of a simpler life. Far away from the hustle and bustle of Big City Life.

(*LIGHTS UP DL. BUD is dressed in priest's robes. ORGAN MUSIC plays.*)

BUD. (*At peace.*) I love being a priest. Everything is so sterile. So serene. The food is so bland. And no one but Father Josiah knows about my mesh bikini pants. (*HE giggles to himself as the LIGHTS go down.*)

SAM. Alan and Vickie ... are still married. In fact, if you were to peek into their home, on any given night, you might see something like this.

(*LIGHTS up DR.*)

ALAN. Chicklets are better than Sen-Sen!

VICKIE. Ah, go choke on your Chicklets.

ALAN. Don't tell me when to choke!

VICKIE. Don't tell me not to tell you when to choke!

ALAN. I'll choke when I damn well feel like it! (*HE strangles himself.*)

VICKIE. You call that a choke? You can't even choke yourself! (*SHE chokes herself.*)

ALAN. Oh, excuse me, Mrs. Heimlich Maneuver. Now you're an expert on choking?

(*THEY continue choking themselves to death as the LIGHTS fade. LIGHTS up on Sam Crumm.*)

SAM. Me? I just travel around now, limping and full of plastic parts. Still a bachelor. But I tell you ... whenever I hear wedding bells, or see a limo with tin cans cruise by while I'm driving down the highway ... I stop. I think back. Remember. Get a little misty-eyed. And try to run the bastards off the road.

CURTAIN

COSTUME PLOT

<u>SAM</u>

<u>ACT I</u>
White Shirt
Grey Slacks
Grey, Pink & Yellow Pullover Sweater
Grey Tie
Black Shoes

<u>ACT II</u>
Same
      into
Yellow Pajamas
Purple & Yellow Plaid Bathrobe
Brown Slippers

<u>MITCHELL</u>

<u>ACT I</u>
Purple Pullover Sweater
White Shirt
Grey Slacks
Black Shoes
      into
Plaid Suit
Plaid Shirt
Striped Tie
White Socks
Black Shoes
      into

Blue Jacket
Kelly Green Pants
Striped Tie
Blue Plaid Shirt
Black Shoes
     into
Cuffed Blue Jeans
Green Plaid Shirt
Red Checked Lumberjack Jacket
Hiking Boots
Fur Elmer Fudd Hunting Hat With Ear-Flaps

ACT II
Same
     into
Grey Prison Stripes

FRAN

ACT I
Knit Pink Dress
Black Boots
Black Belt
Black Bow
     into
First Fat Suit (Additional Fifty Pounds)
Blue Knit Dress
Beige Heels
Red Neck Scarf
Red Purse
     into
Add Additional Tummy Roll to Fat Suit

Floral Moo Moo
   into
Add Additional Thighs and Backside to Fat
Suit
Man's Oversized Overalls
Red Flannel Shirt
Tan Pull-on Boots

ACT II
Same
   into
Thousand Pound Fat Woman Body, Wrapped
in Huge Bath Towel

ALAN

ACT I
Dark Blue Suit
White Shirt
Red Tie
Black Shoes
   into
Print Pajamas
   into
Khaki Pants
Fair Isle Sweater
Loafers
   into
Khaki Pants
L.L. Bean Boots
Flannel Shirt
Jacket

Long John Undershirt
    into
Same, Add:
Green Rain Slicker
Hip Wading Boots
Fishing Hat With Flies

ACT II
Same, Wet Down
    into
Jeans
Red Flannel Shirt
Black Slippers
    into
Blue & White Striped Pajamas
Dark Blue Plaid Flannel Robe
Black Slippers

VICKIE

ACT I
Polka Dot Dress
Matching Bow
Black Heels
    into
Red Satin Pajamas
    into
Blue Skirt
Blue Shoes
Blue Floral Sweater
    into
Black Jeans

Black Boots
Black Purse
Plaid Black & White Shirt
White Cardigan
    into
Same, Add:
Red Rain Slicker
Red Boots

ACT II
Same, Wet Down
    into
Black Jeans
Baggy Grey Sweatshirt
Pink Slippers
    into
White Nightgown
White Slippers
White & Pink Print Robe

HAL

ACT I
Red Striped Pajamas
    into
"Batman" T-Shirt
Baggy Boxer Shorts
"Batman" Hood With Pointed Ears & Eye Cut-
Outs
"Batman" Cape
Green Rubber Boots
    into

Grey Slacks
White Shirt
Grey Tie
Navy Sports Jacket
Black Shoes
Red Sweater Vest
    into
Brown Duck Hunting Jacket
Beige Cords
Blue Sweater
Hiking Boots

ACT II
Same
    into
Blue & White Striped Pajamas
Dark Blue Plaid Flannel Robe
Black Slippers
    into
Grey & Black Prison Stripes

RHONDA

ACT I
Red & White Striped Man's Pajama Top
Red Ribbon in Hair
    into
Long Black Negligee
    into
Hot Pink Negligee
    into
    Soft Pink Ski Sweater

Jeans
Pink Suede Boots
Matching Shoulder Bag

ACT II
Black Negligee
Roman Gladiator Helmet
Beige Slippers
       into
Same, Add:
Gun Belt
Holster
Cowboy Hat
       into
Same, Add:
Matching Robe
Lose Gun Belt & Holster
Keep Cowboy Hat
       into
Pink Fuzzy Robe
Big Fuzzy Slippers

BUD

ACT I
White Duck Pants
Red Polo Shirt
White Tennis Sweater
Loafers
       into
Grey Flannel Slacks
Grey Tweed Jacket

White Shirt
Tie
Black Shoes
    into
Blue Suit
Pink Shirt
Tie
Black Shoes
    into
Brown Cardigan Sweater
Tan Pants
Plaid Plannel Shirt
Dock Siders

ACT II
Short Green Plaid Robe
T-Shirt
Boxers
White Socks
Black Slippers
    into
Priest Robe & Collar
Black Pants
Black Shoes

LINDA

ACT I
White Tennis Skirt
White Polo Shirt
Red Tennis Sweater

White Ankle Socks
White Sneakers
Red Bow
    into
Cobalt Blue Nightgown
    into
Brown Leather Skirt
Cream Sweater With Lace Trim
Cream Boots
Print Scarf on Neck
    into
Blue Jeans
Red Turtleneck
Blue & Red Cardigan Sweater
Red Boots

ACT II
Dark Green Velour Bathrobe
Matching Slippers
    into
Black Leather Storm Trooper Outfit
Hair Slicked Back

PEARL

ACT I
Blue Pilgrim Dress
White Collar
White Apron
White Bonnet
Black Lace-Up Boots

<u>ACT II</u>
Same
     into
White Muslin Nightgown
Night Cap
Black Lace-Up Boots

<u>JEB</u>

<u>ACT I</u>
You're Not In It

<u>ACT II</u>
Revolutionary War Outfit
     into
White Muslin Colonial Shirt
Black Riding Boots
Black Suit

PROPERTY PLOT

Antique Telephone
Apple (One Nightly)
Babies (2)
Bananas (A lot)
Bandana
Baseball Bat, Plastic
Baseball Bat, Wooden
Bat (The Flying Kind)
Bat (Clip-on, Look-alike)
Bear Trap
Bear Trap (Plastic) Used to Clamp on Sam's Foot
Blanket
Book, Thick & Red
Book, Thicker & Red
Bouquet of Flowers
Briefcases (2) (Bud, Mitchell)
Bucket
Bullets
Butterfly Net
Cake (2) (Nightly)
Cake Plates (2)
Cigarette Butt
Corsage
Cut Flowers
Diary, Red
Double-Barrel Shotgun
Dummies (2) "Pearl" & "Jeb"
First Aid Kit
Fishing Rods (2) (Alan & Sam)
Forks (2)

Glass
Guest Register
Hairnet
Hotel Desk Bell
Hub Cap
Ice Bucket
Ice Cream Carton
Keys (5)
Kleenex
Ladder
Ladder (Look-alike) Made with Styrofoam Rungs
Leaves
Lone Ranger Masks (2) (Hal, Alan)
Mallomars
Metamucil
Moose Hunting Coat (With Big Bull's eye on
    Back)
Mug
Overnight Bag (Sam)
Pen
Picnic Basket
Pistol
Power Drill
"Presumed Innocent" (Hardcover Edition)
Pretzel Sticks (Nightly)
Prison ID Numbers (2) (Mitchell & Hal)
Quill
Scarves (2) Silk
Soap Suds
Sponge
Spoon (2)
Stephen King Novel, His Latest

Suitcases (2) (Alan & Vickie)
          (2) (Bud & Linda)
          (1) (Large) (Mitchell & Fran)
          (2) (Hal & Rhonda)
Tomato (Nightly)
Towel
Vase
Watch (Hal)

SET PIECES

Brass Bed
Bureau
Night Table
Park Bench
Wing Chair
Ice Cream Table
Two Chairs
Deacon's Bench
Antique Table
Front Desk
Ladder Back Chair
Miscellaneous Antiques

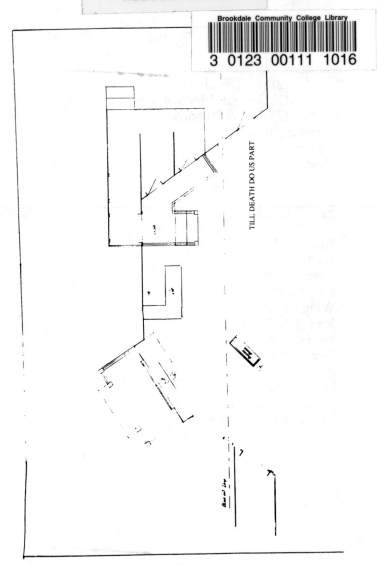

TILL DEATH DO US PART